TRISTAN AND ISEULT

A Cornish love story

Joy Wilson

Bossiney Books · Launceston

This edition published 1999 and reprinted 2001
by Bossiney Books, Langore, Launceston, Cornwall PL15 8LD
First published 1989 as *Cornwall: Land of Legend*
ISBN 1-899383-20-4

© 1989, 1999 Joy Wilson

Front cover photo: AKG London, from a fourteenth century
manuscript *Roman de la Rose* in the Bibliothèque Nationale, Paris

Map by Andrew Jago

Printed in Great Britain by R Booth (Troutbeck Press),
Mabe, Cornwall

Contents

Author's acknowledgements

My sincere thanks are due to all those people who have helped me by providing books, maps and advice. For granting access to interesting sites and allowing photographs to be taken, I would like to thank in particular Mr and Mrs Santo of Lantyan Farm, Mr BV Cock of Goodern, and the lord of the manor of Castle-by-Lantyan. I am grateful to Rev. R Redrup, his son Peter and Mr Donald Curtis for some interesting information about the Tristan legend in St Kea parish. I would also like to acknowledge the help I have received from Charles Thomas, the County Record Office and the Cornish Studies Library at Redruth.

The challenge

There are still secrets to be unearthed in the Cornish countryside. This book records a quest to look for the truth behind a Cornish legend that is known the world over. The great love story of Tristan and his fateful meeting with the Irish princess, Iseult, is full of twists and turns that have caught the imagination of minstrels, poets and writers down through the centuries, and has been retold in many different ways. Richard Wagner was inspired by it to write his great opera *Tristan und Isolde*.

Two of the main characters in the story almost certainly existed in sixth-century Cornwall. When I set out to investigate the evidence still to be found today in the Cornish countryside, I felt tempted to believe that the events on which this dramatic legend was originally based might really once have happened here at the court of King Mark in that remote and distant time.

My main guide through all my explorations was the poem that is probably the earliest version of the story of Tristan and Iseult still in existence. This poem was sung or recited for the first time in Cornwall by an Anglo-Norman minstrel, Béroul, who came here by sea from France some time during the reign of Henry II and his queen, Eleanor of Aquitaine. He made his living by bringing news and entertainment from far away to the people in the isolated wooden castles of his patron, the feudal lord of Cardinham and Restormel in southern Cornwall.

In the poem that Béroul made from this story which he heard from the local people and that so captured his imagination, he recorded the names told to him of the real characters involved, and gave many of the Cornish place-names for the areas through which the lovers travelled in their wanderings. Then he added clear descriptions of the Cornish countryside.

These were the clues that provided me with the challenge to follow them and explore this ancient land from the foot of the Tristan Stone on the Fowey peninsula to the forest of Moresk, to Blancheland and St Michael's Mount, and, finally, from the cliffs at Land's End and Cape Cornwall to look out across the sea towards the Isles of Scilly where Tristan's birthplace, the country of Lyonesse, is said to be submerged beneath the waves.

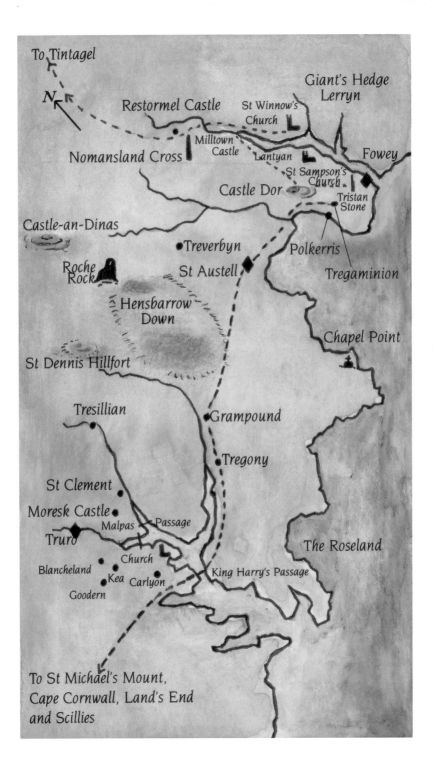

The legend of Tristan and Iseult

Tristan was born a Celtic prince in the country of Lyonesse, long ago submerged under the turbulent sea beyond Land's End. His mother, Blancheflower, was a sister of King Mark who ruled over a large part of Cornwall in the sixth century.

Blancheflower had eloped with the handsome Lord of Lyonesse against her royal brother's will. But unfortunately not long after their marriage her husband was killed in battle. Overwhelmed by her loss Blancheflower herself died just after giving birth to their son. The child remained in Lyonesse in the care of a faithful retainer, Governal. He was christened Tristan which means 'sadness'.

Time passed and the boy grew up a skilled hunter and warrior, and renowned for his harp playing and singing. When he reached early manhood he set out with Governal to seek adventure abroad.

Fate eventually brought their ship to the lands ruled over by his uncle King Mark. Tristan and Governal landed in Cornwall and found their way to Mark's court which was then at the king's main summer stronghold on the great promontory of Tintagel. There Tristan was made welcome and his knightly skills admired.

At this time King Mark's rule over the northern part of Cornwall was threatened by the annual arrival of Prince Morholt, the brother of the Queen of Ireland. He was a ruthless man who demanded an annual tribute from the Cornish. Each year 300 young Cornish men and girls were taken back to Ireland as slaves, together with 300 pounds of silver and of tin.

Not one of the lords assembled at Mark's court had enough courage to challenge Morholt in battle. When Tristan realised this he asked the King to knight him so that he could become the King's Champion himself. He had to reveal that he was the Prince of Lyonesse and also Mark's nephew and so equal in rank to Morholt, whom he challenged in single combat.

King Mark was overjoyed to find his nephew once more, but feared greatly he might lose him in the dangerous undertaking. However, Tristan was determined to fight and destroy the evil Morholt's power over Cornwall once and for all.

The combat took place on the Isle of St Samson a few days later. During a desperate struggle both men were wounded many times. At last, using all his remaining strength, Tristan managed to strike off his enemy's plumed helmet and split open his head with his sword. A small triangular splinter from the edge of the sword blade broke off and lodged in the fatal wound. Felled to the ground, the dying Irish prince was taken back to Ireland by his sorrowing followers. At the Irish court the splinter from Tristan's sword was extracted from the wound in the dead man's head by Morholt's sister, the Irish queen.

The victorious Tristan returned to Tintagel in triumph, where his many serious wounds all healed except one. This was the result of a poisoned spear thrust into his thigh by the treacherous Morholt. The ugly wound festered and there seemed no cure. Its stench was so bad that everyone was driven away except his friend the faithful Governal. Finally, in despair, Tristan asked King Mark for a small boat without sails or oars so that he could drift away on the waves and currents to a distant place where he might find healing.

The vagaries of wind and tide carried the small craft on an erratic course which ended when it beached on a strand in Ireland. As he lay helpless in the boat, all Tristan could do was to draw haunting music from his harp and eventually he attracted the notice of the Irish king.

Without knowing the identity of the wounded knight, the King ordered his daughter, the fair Iseult, to send special herbs to heal Tristan's deadly wound. Such was their power that, as soon as he was restored to health, Tristan left for Cornwall without ever seeing the Princess Iseult or revealing his identity.

King Mark was overjoyed by Tristan's unhoped for return from his mysterious voyage. He resolved to make him his heir, although many of the Cornish lords at court showed bitter hostility to the idea. They put pressure on the king to marry so that Tristan would not inherit the kingdom, but Mark was reluctant. One day in his garden he saw two swallows fighting over a long, shining red-gold hair. He picked up the hair, saying that he would consent to marry only the woman from whose head it had come.

Because of his affection for his uncle, Tristan set out to search for the lady. He wandered far and wide in vain until fate brought him once more to Ireland. He pretended to be a merchant called Tantris, to disguise his links with the Cornish court. At this time the Irish king's fertile lands were being laid waste by a giant snake-like dragon. In utter desperation the king had promised his daughter Iseult's hand in marriage to its slayer. Tristan tracked the malevolent beast to its lair, and after a great struggle he killed it with his magic sword, cutting out its loathesome tongue as a trophy and proof of his deed. But as he wandered back on foot through the ravaged lands he became affected by the tongue's venom and fell to the ground in a deadly faint.

In the meantime the scheming seneschal of the Irish king claimed to have despatched the serpent himself and quickly asked for the princess's hand. But Princess Iseult did not like or believe him and set out to find the true victor. Out in the wastelands she found Tristan lying unconscious. She brought him back to the palace and nursed him slowly back to health.

One day when Tristan was immersed in a wooden bath of water scented with herbs to heal his wounds, Iseult idly drew his sword from its scabbard. There on its blade she saw the triangular notch. She quickly retrieved the fragment of metal that had come from her uncle Morholt's head and found it fitted exactly. Clutching the sword in her hand and blind with desire for vengeance, she ran at the helpless Tristan to take his life in exchange for her uncle's.

But Brangain, her maid and confidante, rushed to restrain her with the warning that if Tristan died Iseult would have to marry the lying steward. Reluctantly Iseult forgave Tristan. By producing the severed tongue of the serpent he was later able to convince the king that he was the true slayer of the beast and in return was offered Iseult's hand in marriage. Tristan accepted, but realising the golden hair that had been the swallows' prize had come from Iseult's head, he claimed her on his uncle's behalf.

True to his word the Irish king agreed, but the queen was anxious that her daughter should not have a loveless marriage with an unknown man. Using all her arts, she prepared a magic love-potion that would last three years exactly. She intended it for King Mark and her daughter on their wedding night.

On the sea voyage home, escorting the Princess Iseult back to King Mark, Tristan became thirsty. He asked for wine to quench his thirst. In her haste Brangain, the maid, accidentally poured the love potion into a single golden goblet. Tristan shared the drink with Iseult and immediately its magic power took effect. From that moment on they had eyes only for each other.

The boat finally reached the Cornish shore and was moored below Port Hern, the Iron Gate, which was the landing place at the foot of Tintagel rock. On King Mark's wedding night Iseult secretly arranged that, under cover of darkness Brangain, a virgin, should take her place in King Mark's bed lest he should discover her own infidelity. The ruse worked and Iseult then quietly assumed her role as queen. The king fell deeply in love with his beautiful Irish bride and was grateful to his nephew Tristan for bringing her to him.

As the summer wore on, Mark's court moved to Lantyan, his castle on a hill near the banks of a great river in the south part of Cornwall. While the king rode out over his lands hunting deer and boar, Tristan and Iseult often met secretly in his chamber. But some of the lords at court had become more envious of Tristan than ever. Gradually they became aware of the illicit liaison between him and Queen Iseult and were quick to inform the king. On one fatal day Mark discovered the two lovers together and exiled his nephew from the court to live in a neighbouring town.

But Tristan and Iseult continued to meet in secret in a nearby orchard at Lantyan. Tristan would throw twigs into a stream running under Iseult's window and, when she saw them, she would hasten to the orchard for an assignation among the safety of the apple trees.

Like many Celtic chieftains, Mark kept a dwarf at court for his amusement, in this case an evil sorcerer called Frocin. Guided by his black magic skills he betrayed the lovers' rendezvous to his master.

So one night, the unhappy Mark went into the orchard and hid on a great oak branch that overhung the stream, intending to eavesdrop on the lovers below. As Tristan approached, moonlight glinted on the surface of the water, revealing a reflection of the king's dark shadow above. Iseult also saw its outline but neither of the lovers made any sign to each other. Both aware of the king's presence, Iseult fiercely reproached Tristan for summoning her from her chamber at so late an hour, while Tristan claimed he had come there only to beg her to intercede with the king on his behalf as a loving nephew. Iseult quickly responded that her love for Tristan was indeed merely a dutiful regard for her husband's nephew.

The lovers then parted, leaving King Mark in his hiding place convinced of their innocence. He vented his anger on the scheming dwarf who temporarily fled the court. So Tristan was reinstated with all his privileges once more. He slept in the king's chamber on a pallet on the floor, as was the custom then for favoured retainers.

One night the king rose at midnight and went off with the dwarf who had used his evil powers to get back into favour. Frocin had laid a trap for the lovers by scattering white flour on the floor between the beds. When the king departed, Tristan sprang from his pallet to the queen's bed in one leap, leaving no footprint. But the exertion opened up a half-healed hunting wound on his thigh and heavy drops of blood stained the queen's sheet. Tristan lovingly clasped Iseult in a close embrace, but then hearing the king's abrupt return with the treacherous dwarf made a desperate leap back to his own pallet. A trail of blood spots stained the flour on the floor: Frocin gleefully held up a lamp to reveal the lovers' guilt to the king.

This time King Mark was unable to forgive. In a violent passion he condemned the two lovers to death. Tristan was to be burned on a huge brushwood pyre already being built on a distant hill. Mark's soldiers dragged him quickly away under heavy guard. On the route to the hill they passed a small lonely chapel built from the stones of the beach out on a rocky promontory by the southern sea. There a hermit kept a light burning to warn mariners of the many jagged rocks concealed at high tide. Tristan pleaded with his captors to allow him to enter the chapel to make a last confession and to pray for his soul. Since it had only one narrow door they allowed him to go in. But in the wall high above the stone altar was a tiny square window filled with rare red glass. Below it outside the fragmented slatey cliff formed a precipice above the restless sea.

Tristan made a sudden bid for freedom. He leapt on the altar and forced the window open. Squeezing his body through the gap he jumped down to a small sloping platform halfway down the cliff. It broke his fall and he was able to scramble sideways down to the beach. There Governal, who had secretly followed on horseback behind the guards, caught up with Tristan as he fled across the sand. He gave Tristan's sword to him as they galloped away from the frustrated pursuers. Ever since that day, according to the story teller, Béroul, the site of the ancient chapel has been known to the Cornish people as Le Saut Tristan – 'Tristan's Leap'.

At first Iseult was also condemned to the pyre, but the great lord Dinas of Dinan, a true friend to the lovers, pleaded successfully for her life. However, in his jealous rage Mark decided on a sordid humiliation of his erring queen. The terrified Iseult was handed over to the uncouth leader of a band of a hundred unsightly lepers. They were all filthy, dressed in tattered grey rags and supported by rough wooden crutches, sounding their doleful clappers to warn people out of their path. Iseult was roughly led away by them towards their group of isolated hovels some distance from the palace near a lonely crossroads.

As they were dragging her through reeds flanking a treacherous marsh, the leper band passed the spot where Tristan was hiding in a thicket with his rescuer. Quickly seizing the opportunity while the lepers were off guard struggling over the wet ground, Tristan rescued the unhappy Iseult from her tormentors.

Then the two lovers, accompanied by the faithful Governal, fled to hide in the great and mysterious Forest of Moresk, which covered a large central area of King Mark's domains. Ordinary people feared to enter this forest and seldom ventured past the thorn trees on its fringe. The two lovers began a fugitive and nomadic life in its shelter.

They were kept alive by Tristan's skill as an archer. They ate venison and nuts from the wildwood, but had no milk or salt or bread. Their only shelter was a bower made of cut branches, with a couch of leaves. Enduring hardship, they remained in the forest growing thin but still obsessed with their fated love for each other.

One day their wanderings led them out of the forest to a distant hermitage built on a lonely granite outcrop overlooking a wild moor. Ogrin the hermit warned them that King Mark had placed a reward of 100 silver marks on Tristan's head. In his piety the holy man urged Tristan to make a confession and repent of his illicit passion. But when Iseult told Ogrin of the love-potion and its irresistible effect he took pity on the pair and allowed them to shelter for one night in the hermitage. Next day for safety the lovers returned once more to their bleak forest existence.

Time passed, and one day when Tristan had been out hunting with his dog Husdant since sunrise, the heat of the hot midday sun beating down on his head caused him to return to their shelter. He stripped to his linen underbritches and lay down to rest beside Iseult who wore only her long chemise. His friend Governal was far afield hunting. A forester happened to pass their grotto and, recognising the pair, rushed off to the court at Lantyan to tell of his discovery.

The woodman's agitated arrival in hope of reward was witnessed by King Mark who ordered him to wait at the foot of the Croix Rouge, a stone cross painted with red ochre that probably marked a boundary near the palace. It stood at a fork in the road where the dead were often buried. There Mark eventually joined him, alone, and the forester led him across country to the lovers' retreat. Stooping low under the boughs as he entered, Mark drew his sword. He saw the lovers lying asleep side by side while between them, unsheathed, was Tristan's bright sword, separating the two. Suddenly the king felt uncertain of their guilt. He was touched by Iseult's frail beauty and, seeing that her wedding ring set with emeralds was loose on her thin hand, he replaced it with the ring she had given him. He removed Tristan's sword and replaced it with his own. Through the leafy canopy overhead a sunbeam flickered over Iseult's closed eyes, burning the delicate skin of her cheek. Mark laid one of his riding gloves across the gap in the branches to shade her from the fierce rays. Then abruptly dismissing his forester guide he rode back to Lantyan.

When the two lovers woke at dusk they were in sad disarray. Iseult recognised Mark's ring and leather glove and Tristan, the alien sword. Until this time the strength of the love-potion had kept the pair aware only of each other and reckless of the their bleak outlaw existence. But soon afterwards, the three years of the potion's fatal power expired. Tristan and Iseult were suddenly overwhelmed by the realisation of the sacrifices they had made to be together, and their treachery to King Mark. They travelled once more to the hermitage on the high rock and asked the hermit to write a letter for them, begging the king's forgiveness. Tristan carried it to Lantyan and Mark was requested to leave his reply tied to the Croix Rouge. Tristan's letter explained that he had sought and found Iseult for the king in the first place, and that when he had later found her helpless in the hands of the lepers he had had no choice but to seek refuge in the forest.

Tristan put himself in great peril when he called the king to the window and thrust the letter into his hand. In due course Mark's reply was hung on the Croix Rouge. He stated that he would take back Iseult as his queen once more, and that in three days time she must meet him at the Gué Aventuros, that is, 'the ford where things happen', otherwise known as the Mal Pas. Tristan was bidden to leave the country of Cornwall altogether.

Ogrin's hermitage? This ancient chapel at Roche was licensed in 1409, but there was a hermitage here before that time, perhaps when Béroul was writing, perhaps even many centuries before that, in the time of Tristan and Iseult

Though the lovers still loved each other deeply, the blind obsession that had bewitched them until now was gone. Quietly they prepared for their parting. Iseult kept their hunting dog, Husdant, and gave Tristan a green jasper ring as a love token. If ever he should need her he was to send the ring and Iseult would come to him at once.

In the meantime Ogrin the hermit had left his windswept hermitage on the high rock and travelled to St Michael's Mount on Iseult's behalf. There at the market, which was held weekly on the sandy shore, he bartered and bought for her a dress of royal purple made of rare Baghdad silk, white and grey furs, and a gentle nag all harnessed in gold. So instead of her drab forest rags Iseult would be regally dressed for the reunion with King Mark at the Mal Pas ford.

When the day came the rich colour of her clothes emphasised the beauty of Iseult's shining red-gold hair and her sparkling green eyes. Sadly Tristan took the bridle of her horse and, leading her across the narrow meadow that sloped down to the Perilous Ford, he solemnly handed her over to the king.

Proudly Tristan said farewell and rode away towards the distant coast. Iseult followed him sadly with her eyes until he was lost to view. Then, once more ceremoniously re-instated as queen, she rode back with Mark to Lantyan.

The next day, she led a grand procession down the paved road to the chapel of St Sampson at the monastery built by the saint under the shoulder of the hill overlooking the wide river below. In the chapel Iseult made a thank offering of a rich embroidered and jewelled robe. Thereafter it was always shown on all the saints' feast days.

That night at the palace at Lantyan the festivities for her return lasted until the moon had waned. Instead of departing across the sea to Brittany as ordered, Tristan went into hiding once more. His refuge was a wooden storage cellar under the house of a humble forester named Orri. There he secretly stayed to receive news of the court and of Iseult's relations with Mark.

It was fortunate that he did so, as some of the unfriendly lords again caused trouble. This time they demanded that Iseult should clear herself of all guilt by undergoing a public Trial by Ordeal. Furious at the lords' enmity, King Mark came to Iseult's side. On seeing him she half fainted, fearing that Tristan's whereabouts had been discovered, until Mark told her of the demand for a trial.

Quick to make a bargain, Iseult said she would be willing to submit to a trial if it was staged at Blancheland, part of Mark's hunting grounds on the high heathland. She requested that King Arthur and his knights should be present as witnesses.

When Mark agreed to this, Iseult sent a secret message to Tristan asking him to come on the day of the trial to the Mal Pas, the ford that led across the river to Blancheland. He was to disguise himself as a leper and to station himself on a rocky mound near the marshy ground where planks were laid across the treacherous river mud.

When the trial day came, Tristan was there on the mound, dressed in the grey rags of a leper and with a begging bowl and wooden clapper to warn the crowds to keep clear. From each person who pushed past him he demanded alms, even from King Arthur and King Mark. Three of the hostile lords came by and demanded directions from the despised leper. Following the way indicated, they wandered sideways into the marsh and sank, only to emerge covered with mud to public humiliation.

But when most of the company had safely negotiated the perils of the Mal Pas, Iseult rode down to the ford. She expertly dismounted and looped her stirrups over the saddle, then, giving her small mount a sharp slap on the rump she sent it trotting delicately across the dark muddy surface to the other side. Near her Tristan in his grimy disguise leaned heavily on his crooked rough-hewn crutch. Iseult approached him and boldly demanded that he carry her across the treacherous ford on his hunchback shoulders. He feigned incomprehension until Iseult ordered him to stoop and clambered up on to his back, urging him across the ford. Tristan lurched unsteadily through the mud, once or twice pretending to stumble. When they reached the foot of the path on the Blancheland side he asked for alms from Iseult as she slid down from his back. But she denounced him as a sturdy rogue and rode her horse up the steep woodland track towards the open heath beyond and the king's hunting lodge.

The next day Iseult had to prove her innocence. Tents were pitched in the high meadow, and the two kings sat in state as witnesses. In front of them on a piece of fine silk cloth were spread all the holy Christian reliquaries from the chapels of Cornwall. Placing her right hand on the most important reliquary of all, Iseult swore a solemn oath before the assembled company. She said that no man had ever come between her thighs save only King Mark, her lawful husband, and the poor leper who had carried her on his back over the dangerous Mal Pas ford. This impressive but ambiguous statement was accepted by all present, and Iseult's innocence was deemed proven.

The great King Arthur returned north once more to his capital of Caerleon in Wales and on to Durham, and King Mark and his queen rode back to the castle at Lantyan. Tristan remained in hiding, but this time he was given refuge in the castle of Dinas in Penwith, by Dinan, his friend among the powerful Cornish lords at Mark's court.

On the surface it seemed that Mark and Iseult were reconciled at last. But as time went on informers disclosed to the king that whenever he was away at his hunting lodge, Tristan was still secretly meeting Iseult. Two evilly disposed lords at court planned to spy on the lovers through a small window of the king's chamber. They hid in a clump of yellow irises on the bank of the stream outside and, using a knife bound on a long stick, tried to draw aside the thin curtain.

Just as Tristan entered the room, Iseult turned towards him and saw the outline of a man's head through the fine linen curtain. She quickly made a sign to Tristan to put an arrow into his bow. Looking up he also saw the shadowy outline and took aim. The swift arrow pierced the man's eye and he fell dead into the stream while his associate fled away in terror. In this way the last of the enemies of the lovers were dispersed, but Iseult realised their troubles were still not over. This time she begged Tristan to leave her and to live far away for his own safety, as Mark would never forgive him.

Tristan finally realised the truth of this. For the safety of them both he had to go. Sadly he took leave of Iseult and sailed across the Channel to Brittany to find refuge.

There, so the Breton legends about Mark and Tristan say, Tristan lived in a royal residence at Carhaix. He passed several years in loneliness, until at last he met a Breton princess also called Iseult: Iseult of the White Hands. Attracted by her rare name and despairing of ever seeing his Cornish Iseult again he took her as his wife. The two lived together in harmony, but because of Tristan's fateful love for the first Iseult, their marriage was never consummated.

In time Tristan was drawn away on many adventures and took part in many battles. Eventually he received a severe wound and in spite of his wife's nursing there seemed little hope of recovery. In despair Tristan asked for the jasper ring to be sent to Cornwall with a message to Iseult the Fair, begging her to come and cure him once more with her healing arts. He ordered that if the returning ship had Iseult on board it was to carry a pure white sail, but if she had refused to come to him then the sail was to be entirely black.

When she received this message the abiding strength of her love for Tristan led Iseult to forsake her husband Mark and the court. She immediately left Lantyan and set sail for Brittany.

Meanwhile Tristan was struggling on the edge of life. His wife tenderly took care of him, but hearing of his first love's approach she gave way to natural jealousy. When the ship appeared on the horizon she reported to him wrongly that it carried a jet black sail.

As the ship beached on the strand, thinking that his true love had in the end failed him, Tristan gave up the struggle to live. As Iseult the Fair walked up the hill into the town she heard all the bells solemnly tolling to mark his passing. With the news that her lover Tristan was dead, Iseult's heart finally broke. She lay down on the pallet beside his lifeless body and died in his arms.

Eventually King Mark arrived in Brittany to seek his wife. He heard at last the full story of the magic love-potion and the fate of the two lovers. Generous of heart and full of sadness, Mark at last understood and forgave the two people he had loved most in the world.

He arranged for the ship to carry the two bodies back to Cornwall. There the lovers were buried side by side with honour and from the two graves sprang two plants, the wild hazel and the yellow honeysuckle, forever intertwined, as they grow still in the hedges today.

One of the delights of exploring the setting of the Tristan legend is that many of the locations are in areas quite unaffected by the twentieth century. I was following the line of the Giant's Hedge when I found this delightful 'signpost' near Lerryn

The Tristan Stone

The great weathered Tristan Stone stands lonely and enigmatic by the side of the road that leads to Fowey town and harbour. Only when the afternoon sunlight slanted obliquely across its granite surface could I make out the small rounded lettering of the sixth-century inscription carved in two vertical columns and very difficult to decipher in its weathered condition. In the Latin of the time it reads:

DRUSTANUS HIC IACIT
CUNOMORI FILIUS

Here lies Tristan,
the son of Cunomorus

Apparently D easily became T in Cornish and so Drustanus is in fact the same as Tristan, while Cunomorus, or Cynwawr, refers to Marcus Cunomorus, King Mark of Cornwall. Tristan was therefore in reality his son.

So through the ages this ancient memorial stone has borne silent witness to the real existence of two of the chief characters of the love story. If Tristan was truly the son of King Mark, perhaps it was the earthy drama of his incestuous love relationship with his father's wife that was remembered and retold many times by the Cornish people. Then a long time afterwards it was heard by the poet who changed the relationship into the more respectable one of uncle and nephew.

Originally the stone stood close to the great earthwork of Castle Dor in a small enclosure by the ancient road that was probably the family cemetery. The stone has been moved many times and I found a 1785 map of Lescrow farm nearby that shows it lying in a field and describes it as at least ten feet high (3 metres), three feet (0.9 m) taller than today. In Tudor times, John Leland, an intrepid traveller in Cornwall, gave its measurements as being a foot (0.3 m) taller than that and wider as well. Intriguingly he also described a third vertical line of inscription on the stone which read:

CUM DOMINA CLUSILLA
with the Lady Clusilla

Clusilla is an Irish name and could be transposed into the rare Cornish name of Eselt. Both are versions of the British 'Ad-silti-a' meaning 'she to be gazed at', and could refer to the golden-haired princess Iseult of Béroul's story.

If the third inscribed line existed it would be called the Tristan and Iseult Stone, and would provide evidence of the existence of all the main characters of the love story. Since the line is not visible today, some scholars doubt that it was ever there. However, looking closely at the stone I could see that a large piece has broken off from the right side - perhaps where the third line was once inscribed.

Still clearly to be seen on the reverse side of the stone, but less often noticed, is a sixth-century T-shaped cross carved in relief. King Mark is known to have been a new convert to Christianity who encouraged St Sampson to found a small monastery at Golant on the King's lands overlooking the River Fowey. The T-shaped cross was also a powerful image used by the pagan Druids who regarded it as the symbol of eternity and often cut sacred trees to the shape of a T. St Sampson had studied Druidic wisdom in his youth in Wales, so perhaps this ancient Christian symbol on the Tristan stone betrays an echo of recently supplanted pagan beliefs in Mark's kingdom. Certainly in later times someone thought it necessary to add a carved cross in a circle high up on the side of the stone, perhaps to sanctify it a little more.

Time and change have not been able to erode the stone's basic message: that once it marked the grave of Prince Tristan, the son of King Mark of Cornwall.

King Mark of Cornwall

In the story of Tristan and Iseult, King Mark has an unenviable role to play as a victim of betrayal and jealousy. But in real life he is well documented as a powerful ruler of sixth-century Cornwall. His name is included in a Dark Age list of the High Kings of Dumnonia who ruled in the Westcountry. There he appears under the title of Cynwawr or, in Latin, Cunomorus, meaning 'large dog'. His other name, 'Marcus', really 'Margh' in Cornish, means 'horse'. Both are sacred creatures in Celtic mythology and so are fit names for a king.

When much of Europe was locked in conflict during the turbulent times of the sixth century, King Mark is recorded as maintaining peace and prosperity in Cornwall. He was an early convert to Celtic Christianity when many of the people on the upland moors still lived in pagan superstition under the sway of the Druids.

Confirmation of his reign and that his main stronghold was in South Cornwall on the Fowey peninsula is given in the life of Saint Paul de Leon, written by a Breton monk. He said that while the saint was in Cornwall, 'his fame reached the ears of King Marc, who is also known by the name of Cunomor, a powerful monarch under whose rule lived people of four different languages. This King desiring to settle firmly and in enduring fashion the foundations of the Christian faith which had only lately been laid in that country and to unite all his subjects in obedience to it... Paul came to the place which in their language is called Caer Bannhed, where now the bones of the same king rest...'

Caer Bannhed, which means 'the high place of the red deer', may have been the original name of the great earthwork fortress of Castle Dor which stands on a hill overlooking the river Fowey in South Cornwall. This windswept place has often been associated with King Mark's palace.

But nearby, in the shelter of the valley below, is the old farmhouse of Lantyan. This is the name of the place which Béroul gave to King Mark's southern citadel. Not far away from here, only a mile or so to the west, is another trace of Mark's links with this area. Overlooking the wide sweep of St Austell bay is the ancient Celtic living site of Kilmarth, which means Mark's Retreat or resting place. There below the old house among its sheltering trees, in a pasture that slopes towards the cliff edge, is a mysterious mound that is said by some to be the grave of King Mark. Certainly from this lonely spot there is an impressive view over what would once have been the king's territories, from the distant moorland of inland Cornwall to the coast and the restless waves of the bay below, with the jagged cliffs around Polkerris and beyond. It seems a fit site for a King's burial place.

On the eastern bank of the River Fowey climbing up a hill above the ancient port of Lerryn, I found another possible link showing King Mark's rule over this part of Cornwall.

From the inlet at Lerryn, across fields and woodland to the West Looe river at least eight miles away, runs a formidable earth and stone barrier crowned with trees, the Giant's Hedge. In places it is still over eight feet (2.5 m) high, with its steepest and most impregnable side facing north. Although the date of its construction is not known – some people attributed it to the work of the Devil – it is much more likely to have been built under the orders of King Mark to defend his territories bordering the Fowey estuary from Irish incursions.

The stormy episode in Cornish history when the Irish made repeated incursions into Cornwall was forgotten until recently when evidence of Irish placenames and carved symbols in stone were discovered here. But long ago the story Béroul recorded told of the sad history of Irish aggression and demands for tin, tribute and slaves that led to Tristan's great fight to the death with the evil Irish lord Morholt. In this way history was preserved in legend.

Polkerris harbour, part of the ancient Celtic living site of Kilmarth, 'Mark's retreat.' The name Mark may be the common Roman name Marcus, since many post-Roman leaders still thought of themselves as Romans; but in the British language the word also meant 'stallion' – a sacred animal

Castle Dor is at its most beautiful in April and May, covered in Spring flowers

Castle Dor

The high earthen banks of the Iron Age hill fort Castle Dor, near Fowey, I have been told, once protected the great wooden palace or feasting hall of King Mark when the stronghold was re-used in the turbulent times of the sixth century.

An excavation carried out in 1936/7 inside the earthwork seemed to confirm this view when an impressive pattern of square postholes was discovered. They indicated that two great halls, a kitchen, granaries and a porter's hut had once stood within the shelter of the high banks. A paved entrance, unusual for the time, was also uncovered, while blue and yellow glass beads and two beautifully moulded fragments of a woman's bangles in green and ultramarine glass were also found. Although they were dated as pre-Roman, these trinkets seemed to confirm a tenuous link with the romantic Iseult story.

Castle Dor's impressive site and spacious enclosure within curved earthen banks first gave me the idea of tracing the Tristan legend in the Cornish countryside. So it was not altogether a welcome discovery to find that archaeologists are now having second thoughts about linking King Mark with Castle Dor at all.

New archaeological analysis of the 1937 finds has completely changed the picture. There is insufficient evidence to prove that Castle Dor was ever used as the residence of a sixth-century Cornish king or of his subjects. The elaborate layout of 'palace' postholes has now been interpreted as only a small complex of humble wooden huts of Iron Age settlements. The extra postholes belonged to stout porches built onto the small huts to keep out the Cornish weather.

Another excavation might change this view, for it is known that many other hill forts in south Cornwall were re-used extensively in the sixth century. It seems strange that Castle Dor, the largest and most impressive of all, was not. Perhaps centuries of deep ploughing of the rich soil in the enclosure have destroyed the evidence.

However, even within the shelter of the great earthen banks Castle Dor would have been a draughty place for a king's palace. Westerly winds blow there throughout the year and the ancient ridgeway which the fort was built to dominate passes uncomfortably close by. For many centuries it was the chief route from North Cornwall to the southern harbours and, like all tracks in Mark's time, it would have been frequented by a sometimes hostile stream of travellers, vagabonds and deserters.

So did the King simply garrison his soldiers and horses up here within its windy shelter to stand guard over the road and keep a watch over the river below and the tidal inlet to the south?

Tintagel

On the great black slate promontory of Tintagel (originally called Pendhu) which dominates that part of the North Cornwall coastline, it is said the legendary fortress of Cornish kings once stood. Tintagel features improbably in the stories of the Arthurian cycle as the great king's legendary birthplace. But it is much more likely to have been King Mark's northern stronghold in his conflict with the Irish, just as recounted in the Tristan story.

Not long ago there seemed little proof of this. On visits to Tintagel all I found were the labelled sites of a small Celtic monastery on the cliff edge, a medieval walled garden and chapel, and the crumbling walls of a twelfth-century castle clinging to the precipitous cliffs; the drama of its position capturing the imagination of every visitor.

But recently new evidence has been discovered that alters the picture of this historic site altogether. When a disastrous fire in the summer of 1983 destroyed fragile plant cover on the western side of the high plateau above the castle site, stone foundations were revealed of over 100 small sixth-century buildings whose existence was quite unsuspected before. This complex of stone outlines in the burnt turf and, possibly more impressive, the discovery of the foundations of a hall over 80 feet (25 metres) long, on the highest part of the plateau overlooking the sea, make it likely that an important sixth-century royal citadel was once sited here. It would have belonged to the kings of the area, if not of the whole of Cornwall, and as one of the high kings of Dumnonia Mark would have ruled from here.

The church of St Materiana at Tintagel is of early Norman construction, but the circular mound around the church encloses a Celtic 'lan', with important sixth-century graves. This is a very ancient and sacred site

On the mainland opposite stands Tintagel church, isolated near the cliff edge and surrounded by its lan or Celtic burial enclosure. Close to it, and much older than the present church, are several impressive grass-covered mounds thought to be the Celtic Christian burial places of once important Dark Age people and rulers. Clearly visible from the promontory, perhaps these graves were the focus of summer rituals held at the Tintagel citadel to reinforce King Mark's ancestral right to rule over his Cornish territories.

If you explore the paths on the promontory your feet are quite likely to uncover a red earthenware fragment from the soil. Many such fragments have been found here; all that remains of large cargoes of amphorae, containers of oil and wine and other luxuries imported in the sixth century from the eastern Mediterranean and North Africa. They were unloaded at the landing place of Port Hern, the Irongate, and carried up the steep paths to the plateau above.

Mark was one of the powerful Cornish rulers who retained the loyalty of the local lords by distributing occasional rich imports of oil and wine. They were paid for by bartering hides and tin streamed from the moors which he had received in tribute from his subjects.

So Tristan would have first come to Mark's court in summertime, when it was assembled at Tintagel in the better weather for royal ceremonies and the landing of rich cargoes in the haven below. From the rocky platform below the Irongate Tristan would have been carried to his boat for the hazardous voyage in search of healing that brought him to Ireland and the fateful meeting with Iseult the Irish princess.

Visitors to Tintagel may find it hard to envisage it as a port, but even in the nineteenth century the cove was regularly used for loading slate from the quarries on the cliffs.

In earlier times, small ships could have moored against the rocks under Port Hern, the Iron Gate, so that supplies could reach the castle by sea.

This is where in the sixth century more than one shipload of oil and wine was landed – indicated by the quantities of broken amphorae on the headland paths.

The photograph shows the later medieval wall which protected the Iron Gate

But as Béroul's story makes clear, and he had probably been told, King Mark's chief feasting hall and palace was not at Tintagel but in a more sheltered setting at Lantyan. There close to the River Fowey he could control his southern Cornish territories and the sea route to Brittany as well.

Lantyan

Two separate narrow high-banked lanes lead down from the Fowey road on the ridge into the valley that lies below Castle Dor. Each drops steeply to the farmplace of Lantyan. At one time the lords of the manor here had jurisdiction over many other manors and land scattered throughout Cornwall, from St Germans to the Lizard.

This spot at a place still known as 'Castle' (which in Cornish meant a hill-fort) is the most likely position for King Mark's summer palace, strategically overlooking the River Fowey

Today at Lantyan the three-storied stone farmhouse, at rightangles to the road, looks out benignly over a secluded garden where the rhododendrons planted at the beginning of the twentieth century have become tall trees.

One of the old farm buildings that are tucked under the shelter of the hill is marked on an earlier ordnance survey map as 'remains of ancient manor house'. Could this have once been part of the ancient palace of King Mark? Certainly the great stones used in its construction and the arrow slits in the walls make it seem very old. But the king's great hall was probably built of wood, and this valley site is too low lying and vulnerable to attack for a sixth-century stronghold.

Behind the farmhouse runs the Saints' Way by which Saint Sampson and other Celtic saints from Wales and Ireland crossed the Cornish peninsula. A little way along, where it skirts the edge of Lantyan Wood and climbs to the top of the hill, I followed it on foot to find the large field which has been called Mark's Gate for as long as can be remembered. From here an ancient track leads through the dense oakwoods down to the edge of Woodgate Pill, a tidal inlet that was once the Fowey River landing place for Lantyan and Castle Dor.

From Mark's Gate through Lantyan Wood I found another way that leads down to the ancient crossing place over the river to St Winnow on the eastern bank. On the hillside behind this Celtic church site there was once a deer park, so these two old tracks from Mark's Gate could once have given access to the King's eastern territories and hunting grounds. From the oakwood shelter of Woodgate Pill Tristan could have sailed downriver and across the southern sea to exile in Brittany.

Reversing my steps I followed the Saint's Way a mile or so inland, passing the hamlet at Milltown to reach the old manor house of Castle sheltered among rare trees.

Several clues seem to point to this place at the head of the Lantyan valley as the most likely site for King Mark's southern palace where many of the events in the love story took place. Castle, or Kestle in Cornish, means a hill-top stronghold. Behind the present manor house stands Great Hill and exploring on the heights I found a gentle south-facing slope with a strategic view over the Fowey river where it curves past St Winnow towards its estuary. Just below this spot there was once a paved ford across to the eastern bank, and to the west across the Lantyan valley, it is possible to see distant Castle Dor and the ridgeway running along the skyline. Looking upstream an alert sentry here could have seen as far as Restormel Castle where an earlier wooden stronghold would have stood, and beyond to the high ground of Bodmin Moor on the distant horizon.

This place was known as Chastell in 1340, but in the Domesday Book and the earliest documents it was Lantyan Parva, part of the great Lantyan desmesne. An old map that gives the field names seems to tell a significant story. There is Castle Meadow, Castle Moor, Hunting Down, and Orchard down by the stream. Rather more sinister is the field close to a turn in the road, called Gallows Down.

Today at the foot of the hill four ancient high-banked roads meet at the bridge over the stream, perhaps an indication that, although remote today, Castle was once a place of importance. The late Georgian manor house is close by, with pointed Gothic windows. A spring flows strongly into a fern-shrouded trough set in the herb garden wall and the house is known to stand on a site where many earlier ones were built in the past. Past the formal garden at the side of the house I followed a track that joins up with another one coming up from the river. Both end abruptly and inexplicably half way up Great Hill. Maybe once they had continued to the site of King Mark's citadel on the hill's southern flank. Only excavation here could provide any proof.

Certainly the sunlit site, the ancient name of Lantyan, the distant hunting grounds and the orchard close to the stream are just as described in the story. Hazel and honeysuckle, the symbols of the lovers, flourish in the Lantyan hedges, intertwined in riotous growth.

St Sampson's Isle and Tristan's Battle with Morholt

Below the site at Castle by Lantyan in the middle of the river Fowey and just before it passes St Winnow church there used to be St Sampson Isle. It is mentioned in a document of 1301. Brother Robert of Pelyn, perhaps a humble successor to St Sampson himself, lived there in solitude. It could well have been the site of Tristan's epic battle with the Irish prince. But time changes river beds, and today at low tide there are only shifting sandbanks at this spot.

The other traditional site for the fight has always been the Isle of Samson in Scilly. There Tristan's struggle with Morholt was believed to have taken place on the sandy flats that lie between the island's two haunted peaks. The stone walls of a very early Celtic hermit's cell were found buried in the sand, and some think St Sampson may have left his monastery at Golant for Lenten meditation here.

St Winnow, seen across the Fowey River from the Saints' Way near Lantyan. In medieval times there was an island just up-river from this spot, called St Sampson's Isle, on which a religious man lived alone. Time has changed the river and now there are only sandbanks. The theme of two heroes fighting on an island is not uncommon in myth

When leprosy was common in Cornwall, anyone affected by the disease lived in a 'lazar' house. Here on the edge of a reedy marsh near Tresillian river (SW 857455) and not far from the ford at Malpas, there used to be such a house. Iseult's choice of disguise for Tristan becomes much more understandable. It was unlikely that members of the Court who might recognise him would approach closely enough to do so

Tristan would have embarked for the Isles of Scilly from Porthleddon beach, the broad harbour. Overlooked by the ruins of St Helen's oratory, and sheltered by the protective bulk of Cape Cornwall, this little beach near St Just in Penwith, although stony and inhospitable today, was once one of the main departure points for direct passage by sea to Scilly.

At the beginning of the twentieth century its fine sand surface was 'dressed' (worked over) for the tin that had been carried on to it from the mining valley of Kenidjack close by. As a result the lighter sand on the beach was washed away out to sea, leaving it rocky and useless as a harbour, and the sand has never returned.

The Band of Lepers

According to Béroul's story, there was a leper at Lantyan. He was leader of a band of comrades, a hundred strong, to whose grimy refuge King Mark handed over poor Iseult. Later in the story, at Iseult's suggestion, Tristan adopts the disguise of a leper for the important encounter at Malpas Ford.

At one time leprosy was rife in Cornwall, brought by sea-traders from the East. Only a mile or two away from Lantyan, not far from No Man's Land crossroads on the Lostwithiel road, there was a lazar house called Maudlin set in a remote field. So it is likely that there were lepers at Lantyan in King Mark's time. Legally declared dead to the world, they wore rough homespun and held a stick to support diseased limbs. They carried a bell to give warning and a wooden cup for alms. Small humanity was shown to them and there was little medical help. No wonder they were often depicted as repellent and of uncertain temper.

On the edge of a reedy marsh near the Tresillian river not far from Malpas there used to be another lazar house. It stood at Kiggon, near Truro, and from there a leper could easily have taken the river path that leads by St Clement to Malpas Ford. So Tristan's choice of disguise was not so strange after all.

Tregaminion Cross – Croix Rouge

This cross once stood on the boundary of Castle by Lantyan. So it seems possible that it was the Croix Rouge of Béroul's story on which the messages between Tristan and King Mark were hung. Red ochre was often applied to crosses and signposts to make them stand out.

St Clement, a delightful spot only a mile from Truro (SW 850439), can be reached by road or by the footpath from Tresillian to Malpas, through the 'Forest of Moresk' and beside the Tresillian River

Tregaminion Cross, which may be the Croix Rouge, at Tregaminion Church (SX 096519). This cross is not to be confused with a cross-head which faces you as you approach the church, but can be found to your right – sometimes deeply hidden in the undergrowth, sometimes visible, depending on the current upkeep of the churchyard

Tregaminion Cross has a chequered history. At the time of the Black Death a troop of wandering flagellant monks paused beside it and, to atone for the people's sins (thought to have caused the plague), they scourged themselves into a frenzy. A long time later the cross was uprooted and used as a footbridge over a stream. Then it was rediscovered and sold for £5 and taken to Devon. Just a fortnight later it was claimed back by the Rashleigh family who set it up in an octagonal base of unknown origin with a strange zigzag and dot design. They placed it in Tregaminion churchyard not far from Kilmarth on the Fowey peninsula. There I found it half hidden by giant rhododendrons, with the damage suffered from the feet that once passed over it clearly to be seen.

Orchards in Lantyan

When much of this part of Cornwall was forested, harbouring wild boar and an occasional wolf pack, and the rest was wild heathland or open moor, the walled enclosure of an orchard with short grass underfoot and the shade of apple-hung branches provided a perfect trysting place for lovers.

For a long time there was a large orchard at Castle, not far from where the stables are today. The stream flows nearby and trees overhang it, just as in the story when King Mark concealed himself on a branch above the water to eavesdrop on Tristan and Iseult's clandestine meeting in the shelter of the apple trees.

Until comparatively recently the Fowey river was renowned for the many orchards along its banks or on farms nearby. The apples were grown for food or cider, and were often given in lieu of wages. The hillsides sloping towards the river allowed any frosty air to drain away to the valley below and so were ideal for growing fruit.

St Sampson at Golant

The church of Saint Sampson looks out over the sandy tidal reaches of the River Fowey, standing on the hill above the village and harbour of Golant. It was to this church that, legend tells, Iseult rode in a procession with coloured flags flying, along a paved road from Lantyan. She brought as a thank-offering for her reconciliation with King Mark the rich gift of an embroidered robe in silver and gold. It became a treasure of the church for centuries to come.

But in Iseult's time all that was here was St Sampson's little round hut and those of his few monks. They were probably built of reed and cob, grouped round the holy well still here today beside the church porch. Sampson's chapel of wattle or local wood is thought to have occupied a small area where the present chancel stands. Enclosed within the oval earthen bank, this would be the extent of the little Celtic monastery founded by the saint to help convert the people to Christian beliefs.

Perhaps appropriately, only on Sunday is it permitted to walk along the railway track to locate the cave that was once St Sampson's refuge beside the river. Holy men in Celtic times liked to immerse themselves in freezing water as an aid to penance, prayer and meditation, and so Sampson chose this cave close to the river.

Under a thick curtain of creeper I found it hard to locate in the fractured rock of the hillside. But inside, exactly as it is described in St Sampson's 'Life', water drips continually and uncomfortably from the roof and splashes down on the big stones fallen to the pebble covered floor. It is not hard to believe the story that Sampson was forced to vanquish a dragon which lived in its depths.

The church of St Sampson at Golant. The present building was consecrated in 1509 but replaced earlier buildings on the same site, and in King Mark's time there would have been no more than a few simple huts forming St Sampson's monastery. The holy well outside the church door may have been there even before St Sampson arrived

The Hermitage of Roche Rock

When Tristan and Iseult eventually wandered away from their woodland refuge in search of nourishment, they came by chance upon the solitary hermitage of Ogrin the holy man. The lovers returned twice to him to seek forgiveness and prayers for their well being, and in time Tristan used Ogrin's skill in letter writing (rare at that time) to communicate with the estranged King Mark at Lantyan.

The Forest of Moresk used to extend far into the hinterland and from its borders the erratic wanderings of the two lovers, on the wild moorland that extended beyond it, might well have brought them to the foot of Roche Rock. It is known that in very early times there was a hermitage, perhaps the first in Cornwall, on the summit.

Roche Rock is a solitary outcrop on the edge of the high downs that lie between Bodmin and St Austell town. The gaunt and tumbled mass of black granite and quartz rises abruptly out of the surrounding moorland, and the sight of its high jagged outline in dark silhouette against the western horizon can arouse awe in those who pass on the roads nearby.

When Christianity was first brought to Cornwall by Celtic saints from Wales and Ireland, a small oratory was built between the two highest pinnacles of Roche Rock. It was constructed in a space hollowed out of the rock face, with rough walls made from random stones gathered up from where they lay in the bracken below. Water came from a small spring among the boulders, and in this draughty shelter there lived a long succession of dedicated holy men whose solitary prayers helped to sanctify the place. Ogrin the hermit may well have been one of their number.

At the end of the Middle Ages, a more elaborate hermitage was built here with walls of quarried ashlar stone strong enough to withstand the winds of centuries. The chapel, with an east-facing window, was constructed on top of the original rock-hewn hermit's cell that had always been reached by a precarious wooden ladder. It was dedicated to the Archangel Michael, long known as the saint of high places and the vanquisher of evil forces.

Marazion – possibly the most ancient town in Cornwall, where tin was traded more than 2000 years ago. In the ancient folklore of Cornwall, Marazion features as the largest town in the far West. Boats were drawn up on the beach. In stormy weather, they took cover in the lee of the Mount

The market at St Michael's Mount

Ogrin the hermit would have had a long journey on foot over wild country to reach the market at St Michael's Mount. He wanted fine clothes of silk and ermine for Iseult to wear for the reconciliation with her husband, King Mark.

Marazion (Marghas-byghan) means 'little market' in Cornish, and a 'Thursday market' was also held on the sandy strand opposite St Michael's Mount for hundreds of years. Cornish ingots of tin, hides and wool were bartered for luxury goods brought from afar by sea-traders from the eastern Mediterranean and France.

Ogrin might well have found silk for sale here, but the cloth would have been extremely expensive because of its rarity. During the sixth century a few silkworm eggs were stolen and illegally smuggled out of China to the merchants of Byzantium. Once the great Chinese secret of silk-making was learnt by them, Byzantium and Baghdad held on to the monopoly for 500 years. Silk was so rare in western lands that the cloth made from it was reserved for royalty alone to wear. Iseult's fine dress of deep purple silk and ermine would have been a truly regal garment at a time when the best clothes available for even the most prosperous in Cornwall were simply made of fine linen or wool.

All goods exchanged by barter at the markets of Marazion would have been landed or shipped from the harbour in the shelter of the Mount, whose history as a port may go back to prehistoric times.

St Michael's Mount seen from Marazion

Chapel Point, near Mevagissey (SX 029434) – the site of 'Tristan's Leap'?

Tristan's leap and escape from his captors

On the way by which they went
A chapel on a hill
Was built on a rocky pinnacle
It overlooked the sea in the north-east wind.
The part called a chancel was built on a mound
Beyond was nothing but the cliff
The hill is smooth slatey rock
If a squirrel jumped from there
It would be killed I guarantee ...

Béroul, *The Romance of Tristan*

This seems to be an almost exact description of Chapel Point, a long sea-girt promontory quite close to Mevagissey harbour on the opposite shore of St Austell Bay to the Fowey peninsula and Lantyan.

Perhaps Béroul saw Chapel Point on his voyage from France, for he must have landed somewhere on this stretch of Cornish coast. Certainly he stated in his poem that 'from time immemorial the country people have called this place Tristan's Leap.'

It might have been this well-known story of Tristan's escape that inspired Sir Henry de Bodrugan to make a similar escape from near the spot a few centuries later. Lawless and piratical, Bodrugan owned all the land here and lived in a fortified manor house at the head of the valley nearby. When his fortunes finally waned and the tide of kingly politics turned against him, he made a daring escape from his enemies by jumping his horse down the cliff near Chapel Point to reach a waiting ship that carried him to safety and exile overseas.

From Colona beach on the west side of Chapel Point, if you look up towards the summit of the promontory, a small level platform is visible beneath the trees in the garden of the middle house built there. Forming part of a rockery a few courses of foundation walls remain. They are all that is left of an ancient 'Lighthouse' chapel that stood here in medieval times on the exposed rock summit of the promontory. In this lonely place a hermit tended a flickering light that shone out seawards through the narrow chapel window. For centuries it was a warning to seafarers of the dangerous submerged rocks off the end of the point.

The Forest of Moresk – a day's ride from Lantyan

The southern route through Cornwall from Plymouth and upcountry crosses the narrow bridge over the Tresillian river where the last skirmish of the Civil War took place. Then after passing through Tresillian village, leaving the tidal mudflats of the river behind, the road climbs a long winding hill before gently descending into Truro.

Either side of the busy road old oak trees can be seen growing in scattered patches. Their crooked branches only half conceal the serried ranks of a modern conifer plantation. The hardwood trees are the last remnants of the great Forest of Moresk which once covered all this part of Cornwall and is mentioned in the Domesday Book.

Oak, ash and hazel have probably grown here since the days of the prehistoric wildwood, and over the years they have provided fuel and charcoal for the local population, timber for their homes and ships, oak bark for tanning, and acorns to feed the pigs. Deer also used to roam in the forest, which made it a privileged hunting ground for the early Cornish kings, probably including King Mark himself.

For those who were not afraid to enter it, the forest could provide a rough shelter – Tristan and Iseult are said to have sought refuge in Moresk.

Where the main road finally leaves Tresillian village I found a little gap in the hedge. It opened onto a signposted public footpath that follows the ups and downs of the Tresillian river bank all the way to Malpas Passage. It starts by skirting the edge of the reedy marsh close to where the lepers of medieval times once lived in isolation at Kiggon. After continuing around Pencalenick Point it then climbs slightly uphill, and I followed it in the shade of the forest's ancient oaks.

Past the small river landing place with its boats below the old church of St Clement, the path goes around the foot of Dinas Hill. Near the clump of trees on its summit is the site where Moresk Castle once stood. There must have been an earlier Celtic fortification here, perhaps a wooden watchtower which would have commanded the extensive and strategic view up river and eastward over the royal territories towards Lantyan. Downstream towards Malpas Passage a watch could have been kept on the ancient ford with its dangerous crossing over the Truro river to Blancheland on the southern bank.

Above: The ford at Malpas, seen from the end of the ancient track from Blancheland. Malpas today is a suburb of Truro. At this point the Truro River is joined by the Tresillian River, and there was until recently a small three-way ferryboat, which had replaced the ancient and dangerous ford

Opposite: Old oak trees are the last remnants of the great Forest of Moresk which once covered a large part of Cornwall, the central area of King Mark's domains. Tristan and Iseult took refuge in this ancient forest, a wild and mysterious place which few dared to enter.

A lovely walk alongside the Tresillian River, through what remains of the forest, is described on page 38

Malpas – 'the ford where things happen'

Mal Pas means 'bad place', or 'treacherous ford', and it can still be found in Cornwall today. Just south of Truro in tiered rows on the hill the houses and cottages of the small village of Malpas look out towards the place where Tresillian creek and the Truro River meet between heavily wooded banks on the Blancheland and Roseland sides. They merge later with the waters of the Fal.

The hazardous Mal Pas ford of Béroul's story over which Iseult was carried by Tristan, disguised as a leper, is described as a series of narrow planks laid on the mud to reach to the Blancheland shore. Straying from the right place, three of the unfriendly lords were engulfed by the mud. Certainly at this place today such a crossing on foot would be quite treacherous. Perhaps in earlier times the Truro river was shallower and the mud flats less extensive and treacherous, but the crossing to Blancheland must have been always a Mal Pas, a dangerous ford.

These days the Falmouth steamers moor in summer at the landing stage and there is an occasional foot ferry to the Roseland bank. Small boats bob at anchor in the current all the year. But when the tide in the river ebbs and only a ribbon of water is left, a dramatic change takes place. Extensive shining mudflats are revealed, strewn with bladderwrack and tidal debris, a haunt of sea birds and waders. To cross here is certainly not a safe undertaking: it has been negotiated by only a careful few using tidal calculations and protective clothing.

In Malpas village several old paths approach the little waterfront which must once have been the ancient fording place to cross the river. The old road that follows the river bank from Truro meets the footpath I took from Tresillian which leads past the village of St Clement and Moresk castle, while from the top of the hill above Malpas village an ancient track, not much used now, still leads down towards the water. All these routes must have been used by early travellers to reach this important crossing place.

Blancheland

Opposite Malpas village on the far river bank the oak trees grow close together and their sturdy branches lean down to the water. An ancient hollow way, worn deep in the rock, leaves the shore and climbs steeply uphill through the trees. At its foot there is an immense boulder on the edge of the mud on which Tristan might have stood to say farewell when Iseult leapt down from his back after fording the river. She may have urged her horse up this very trackway through the woods to reach King Mark's hunting lodge in Blancheland where her ordeal by holy relics was to take place.

Today the area south-west of Truro above the river is St Kea parish. It includes a wide stretch of territory with fertile lands close to the river, and scrub and heath on the uplands beyond. The name Blancheland is not found on any modern map, but in the heart of Kea parish an avenue of trees leads towards an old farm called 'Chyrwin'. It is built on the site of an original Celtic homestead, just where the rich pastureland gives way to the higher heath. The ground is widely scattered with fragments of white quartz and 'Chyrgwin', and 'Alba Landa' on old documents means White Down, the Blancheland that was once the royal hunting ground.

The track Iseult followed from the river leads to a lane that passes close to the narrow ruined tower of old Kea church. It stands in trees above the tidal inlet where St Kea first moored his boat after his voyage to Cornwall from Glastonbury. St Kea fell foul of the local ruler Teudar, a predecessor of King Mark, when he sheltered a frightened stag fleeing from the royal hunting party. In a wild rage King Teudar knocked out one of the saint's teeth, and in later times the holy well of St Kea became a favourite resort for toothache cures. Teudar repented of his fit of bad temper and encouraged the saint to found a small Celtic monastery in this fertile area.

Once up on the high ground, heath, rough pasture and old mineworkings stretch along the horizon as far as Chacewater, which means 'the hunting ground near water'. This must surely be a clear indication that this part of Blancheland was once the great hunting territory of the Cornish kings.

Not far away in the corner of a large level meadow with a commanding view over the surrounding country I found an impressive

After crossing the ford on Tristan's back, Iseult mounted her horse and rode up a steep woodland track towards the open heath.

The route Béroul had in mind can still be found, though now it is an overgrown footpath through woodland.

To find this beautiful spot, take the Falmouth road from Truro, and turn left to Old Kea. The path leaves the lane at SW 845422 and heads north to the ford

rectangular earthwork, its enclosing earthen banks defined by the twisted thorn trees that grow on them. This is Goodern and old documents speak of the place as having once been a 'castle' of irascible King Teudar who fought a battle against Christians here. During the battle he fell from his horse and was killed, and may have been buried under a large tree-crowned barrow which stands close by. Teudar's Christian successor King Mark is thought to have used Goodern as a hunting lodge. And in the level meadow alongside, perhaps the tournament and Iseult's Ordeal witnessed by the kings were staged.

An odd footnote is provided by an historian who tells how in Tudor times a local farmer dug up at Goodern enough gold and silver to transform him from peasant to gentleman.

Tredruston and Hryt Eselt

A lonely signpost at a crossroads near Wadebridge in North Cornwall points down a narrow wire-fenced road leading to Tredruston – a Cornish Celt named Druston (or Tristan) once built his homestead on this sheltered valley hillside below St Breock Down. The signpost provides silent proof that Tristan was a personal name used in very early times in Cornwall, although it was almost unknown elsewhere. This Celtic farmer may have been called after a local prince whose illicit love story had become part of folklore.

At least a hundred years before the poet Béroul came to Cornwall, the people who lived on the wild Lizard peninsula knew all about Princess Iseult's adventures. In a Charter of 976 AD a land boundary near St Keverne was defined. It included a remote crossing place over the little Porthallow river which was called Hryt Eselt, the Cornish for 'Iseult's Ford'. This is the only record of the name Iseult, which at that time was quite unknown outside Cornwall. It was not until much later that the lovers' story, first heard in Cornwall, captured the imagination of poets all over Europe.

If you explore the lattice-work of lanes between Goonhilly Down and St Keverne, you will find Eselt's Ford (SX 774218). A lane of medieval narrowness, once a packhorse trail, runs steeply downhill and crosses the river flowing down the valley below Lesneague farm. From a perilous perch on the riverbank I could see the large granite slabs of the original clapper bridge, now quite concealed under the tarmac road surface. In its time it must have replaced the slippery stepping-stones of Hryt Eselt, the little ford of Celtic times.

These old farm buildings at Lantyan (SX106573) are probably the remains of the medieval manor house. Even these buildings are much too recent to have formed part of King Mark's palace, which was in any case probably at Castle

Pendinas, St Ives

Dinan, Tristan's friend at King Mark's court, owned the fortified stronghold on this headland, the 'Island' whose bulk protects the fishermen's and artists' cottages of Downalong St Ives. Leland stated in his *Itinerary* of 1537 that Pendinas fort was 'built on the peninsula and stony rok where now the town of St Ives stondeth', and it defended the sandy landing place below.

Dinan refused to ally himself with the jealous Cornish lords and gave secret shelter to Tristan when he was exiled from court. His friendly nature was also shown to the Christian Irish princess St Ia, who, it is said, after making a hazardous voyage from Ireland on an outsize leaf, landed on Porthmeor beach below his stronghold. In truth St Ia's 'leaf' was probably a greased hide and wicker coracle, an unfamiliar craft to Cornish eyes. St Ia persuaded Lord Dinan to build her an oratory close to the sea where the parish church stands today. Her holy well is still to be found near Porthmeor beach where her first baptisms were made.

Tristan's Land of Lyonesse

Stories of a lost land persist in West Cornwall where the ancient name for Land's End was Pedn an Laaz meaning 'end of the earth'. Folk memories still remain of a beautiful and fertile land called Lyonesse that once existed beyond Land's End and Cape Cornwall, extending as far as the Isles of Scilly and south towards Mount's Bay.

All the versions of the love story state that many centuries before the fatal cataclysm which is said to have overwhelmed it, Prince Tristan was born in Lyonesse and that it was his by inheritance.

On an old seventeenth-century map printed in Holland I found some evidence that Tristan's land of Lyonesse could have been a reality. The Seven Stones on which the Wolf Lighthouse stands today beyond Land's End are marked on the map as 'The Gulfe' with a Latin inscription which reads 'A land which sank having previously been exposed above the sea'. The Seven Stones are thought to be the tip of an extinct volcano and the Sennen fishermen used to speak of a city called Tregva or Lyons that once stood in its shelter. They told tales of doors and windows they had dredged up in their nets.

Very much earlier, in the *Anglo-Saxon Chronicle*, a monk from Worcester confidently wrote that all the land here was totally destroyed on 11 November 1099. On that night, by the light of the new moon (often a time of storm in Cornwall) a surge of tempestuous sea 'overflowed the shore and destroyed many persons and innumerable oxen and sheep'.

Today in Mount's Bay, near Penzance, when the sea recedes further than usual at stormy times of the year, witnesses have seen and even photographed the blackened and spongy remains of large tree stumps with their root systems still embedded in the sand. Robert Hunt the folklorist, who collected so many Cornish legends and stories in the nineteenth century from the people of Penwith, left a true account of how, as a schoolboy in Penzance, he and some friends had walked far out over the wet sands at extreme low tide. There they found tree trunks with fragments of leaves and beech nuts still preserved around them in the sand. He thereby confirmed the *Anglo-Saxon Chronicle* account in that the great inundation which destroyed a beech forest must have happened after a fierce autumn storm when the trees were still in leaf and bearing nuts.

In 1835, a former lakebed was exposed in similar conditions near Newlyn at Gwavas Point. Surrounding it were traces of marshy ground and trees. But most mysterious of all was a dug-out canoe found with an ancient coin embedded under the remains of a mast. This primitive craft must once have floated on a shallow freshwater lake, separated by marsh and woodland from the open sea.

Until now this scattered evidence of a sunken land off Cornwall has been taken lightly or even quite discounted. But recent archaeological discoveries on the Isles of Scilly do confirm that a dramatic submergence of land did take place when a destructive ocean surge occurred, perhaps caused by an earthquake, in early medieval times. On some of the islands, including Samson, primitive man-made stone walls lead away from the land and continue on under the sea. Submerged burial cists and remains of huts have also been found, washed over by the sea today. All are evidence of a submerged central fertile plain that once joined all the islands into one.

The end of the story

Breton legends still exist telling of the many exploits there of a local ruler Marc'h, also known as Conorre or Conomorus. So did King Mark who ruled over a large part of Cornwall also have jurisdiction over territories in southern Brittany? Place names in Brittany which feature in the story such as Carhaix, Tristan's home in exile, and Penmarc'h in Finisterre where the lovers met their tragic fate, could be clues to this. The legend states that King Mark in compassion ordered that the bodies of the lovers united in death were to be brought back to Lantyan and buried there in the same grave. Today not far from Lantyan, the Tristan memorial stone still bears silent witness to the truth behind the legend.

Bibliography

Béroul, *The Romance of Tristan* (Penguin, 1985)

Ditmus, EMR, *Tristan and Iseult in Cornwall* (Forrester Roberts, 1965)

Doble, Canon Gilbert, The Saints of Cornwall series: *St Sampson, St Paul Aurelian* (1960)

Ewart, A (ed), *The Romance of Tristan* (French text) (Bristol, Classical Press, 1991)

Henderson, Charles, *Essays in Cornish history* (Bradford Barton, 1963)

Loth, Prof. J, *Contributions a l'étude des romans de la table ronde* (Paris, 1912)

Mandach, André de, *La légende de Tristan au moyen âge* (Kummerle Verlag, 1982);
The shrinking tombstone of Tristan and Isolt (Journal of Medieval History, 1978)

Padel, Oliver, *The Cornish background to the Tristan stories* (Cambridge Medieval Celtic Studies, Summer 1981)

Quinnell, Henrietta and Harris, Daphne, *Castle Dor: The chronology reconsidered* (Cornwall Archaeological Journal, No. 24, 1985)

Thomas, Charles, *Exploration of a drowned landscape* (Batsford, 1985);
The Book of Tintagel (Batsford, 1993)